write, from the beginning

Nathan Levy

write, from the beginning

by

Amy Burke and Nathan Levy

N.L. ASSOCIATES, INC. - PUBLISHERS
P.O. Box 1199
Hightstown, New Jersey 08520

N.L. Associates, Inc., Revised Edition 2004
Original Copyright © 1987 by N.L. Associates, Inc.

ISBN 1-878347-54-3
Formerly ISBN 0-8290-0993-0

Printed in the United States of America

For my family...
my husband, Barry and
my children, Rachel Elisabeth
and Seth Evan

table of contents

Introduction   i.

A Note On Structure   iii.

I. Right At the Start (Skill-Building)   1

II. Getting To Know Me (What I Think)   23

III. Explorations (Discovering Others and the World)   47

IV. Imagination (Tradition With A Twist)   61

V. Mystery Chapter (One-of-a-Kind Assignments)   75

INTRODUCTION

Write, From the Beginning suggests a "positiveness"
about the teaching of writing to young students. Children
in the lower grades have much to say (and write about) in
terms of themselves and their world, and they need to be
presented with the opportunity to do so. Too often, they
have been limited by traditional formats (THE composition)
and stereotypical topics deemed suitable for youngsters
(summer vacations, talking animals, and favorite pets).
The writing material contained in this book is an attempt
to break away from tired assignments and formats. The pur-
pose of the exercises is to initiate an interest in writing.
Afterall, "wanting to" is the initial step in learning.

The exercises arose out of my need to provide lower
grade students with writing experiences that 1-would speak
to children as young people with valid opinions and ob-
servations, 2-would get them writing without tiring them
out (the writing of one sentence for a second grader can
sometimes be a monumental task), 3-would blend fantasy
and introspective exercises (dealing with self, others and
the world), 4-would value and foster critical thinking, and
5-would offer variations on a theme (many of the exercises
consist of three or four different writing activities) to
provide fexibility and OPTIONS for the wide range of ability
levels found in the classroom.

The material is specifically designed to be read (and
acted upon) by most second-fourth grade students. The
exercises can be duplicated and distributed for independent
use or they can be discussed effectively in either small
groups or as a class. Students are asked to make lists, use
the library, complete sentence stems, answer questions,
write stories, take surveys--all means to an end, requiring
different levels of skills and different amounts of writing
for every ability students.

As a teacher of creative writing, you have basic methods
that work for you. What I offer, is the material with which
to implement your writing program. The assignments are
constructed so that the content of the responses is never
programmed, rather they are meant to foster a more personal
and creative writing experience. Their structural
similarity to activity cards purposefully provides flex-
ibility for the student. Depending on ability level, students
can be assigned all or some of the activities on a particular
page, or might be allowed to choose for themselves. In any
event, within most assignments, there is something for

everyone. I have also tried to capitalize on the interest that young students have in the world around them, in the ideas of others, in the way they perceive themselves, in the things they have yet to explore or understand.

The transfering of private thoughts onto paper is a fragile and complicated process; wanting to do so has to come from within. To get children writing is to first get them thinking--in new ways, about different things. When that time comes, it is important that both you and your students find that ALL writing...is creative.

A NOTE ON STRUCTURE

The writing exercises in this book are based on the convention of the sentence. While I feel it is realistic for children in the lower primary grades to be exposed to "formal paragraphing," it is not practical to expect very young writers to deal with topical development and the cohesiveness necessary for paragraphing while still struggling to spell words and compose simple sentences.

Therefore, the writing assignments are primarily designed to provide students with the opportunity to use newly acquired sentence writing skills. It is important to realize that a "story" for a first-grader can be a few well-constructed sentences and is the equivalent of a five or six paragraph theme in the upper grades. The more a child "practices" writing sentences, the more likely s/he will be willing to tackle paragraphs later on. First, allow the student to become comfortable with his/her thoughts. Slowly and carefully, these ideas can be guided into gramatically correct and complete sentences. Obviously, the more a child wants to write, the easier the whole process becomes. My advice is to let it happen naturally. It is essential that children do not become intimidated by the writing PROCESS and give up. For that reason, many of the exercises ask students to make lists. Aside from the organizational benefits, lists are an easy and tireless way to get kids writing--word by word. The next step, when a child indicates to you that s/he is secure enough to proceed from "word" writing, is to develop one or two of the words on a particular list into sentences. The progression is a simple and natural one.

Writing is like a jigsaw puzzle. Children need to put the pieces together to find out what it's all about. Sentence writing is a necessary and important piece of that puzzle. Skill building and creative expression CAN go hand in hand, if taken one step at a time...right, from the beginning.

I. Right at the Start

Skill Building...

it's all about you...

One of the best things to write about is yourself; it's amazing how much more you learn about yourself when you write it down. The next few pages will give you some ideas to write about. Please go into as much detail as possible when finishing these sentences.

The most exciting thing I ever did was _____

_____

_____

_____

_____

_____

_____

The scariest thing that ever happened to me was

_____

_____

_____

_____

_____

_____

My favorite sport to participate in is

_____

_____

_____

_____

_____

_____

_____

The sport I most enjoy watching is

_____

_____

_____

_____

_____

Of all the famous people in the world, my favorite is

_____

_____

_____

_____

_____

_____

_____

_____

If I could go anywhere in the world, I would go to

_____

_____

_____

_____

_____

_____

My own personal hero is _____

_____

_____

_____

_____

_____

_____

_____

The hardest I remember laughing was when

_____

_____

_____

_____

_____

_____

_____

The saying I use most often is "_____

_____

_____

_____

_____

_____

_____

If I had the opportunity to host my own talk show, the three people I would choose to be my guests are

_____

_____

_____

_____

_____

_____

_____

_____

_____

_____

_____

I love my parents because _____

_____

_____

_____

_____

_____

_____

My favorite animal is the _____

_____

_____

_____

_____

_____

_____

My favorite part about going to school is

_____

_____

_____

People see me as _____

_____

_____

_____

_____

_____

_____

_____

my favorite story ...

1- What is your favorite story? Why is it your favorite?

2- Who is your favorite character in the story? Write some sentences that start:

_____ is my favorite character because _____.

3- Does your favorite character remind you of anyone that you know?

4- What are some of the things your favorite character does that you would like to do?

what's in a name?

Write **4** names for each category:

Old Fashioned Names

1. _____
2. _____
3. _____
4. _____

Science Fiction Names

1. _____
2. _____
3. _____
4. _____

Heroic Names

1. _____
2. _____
3. _____
4. _____

Villainous Names

1. _____
2. _____
3. _____
4. _____

Fairy Tale Names

1. _____
2. _____
3. _____
4. _____

Hollywood Names

1. _____
2. _____
3. _____
4. _____

SCARFACE   MERLIN   Rebekah   LANCE   Elizabeth

Choose **1** name from your list of "Old Fashioned Names" and describe that character.

Name of character: _____

Descriptive Words:

1. _____ 4. _____
2. _____ 5. _____
3. _____ 6. _____

Choose **1** name from your list of "Science Fiction Names" and describe that character.

Name of character:
Descriptive Words: _____

1. _____ 4. _____
2. _____ 5. _____
3. _____ 6. _____

Choose **1** name from your list of "Heroic Names" and describe that character.

Name of character: _____
Descriptive Words:

1. _____ 4. _____
2. _____ 5. _____
3. _____ 6. _____

11

Choose **1** name from your list of "Villainous Names" and describe that character.

Name of character: _____

Descriptive Words :

1. _____ 4. _____
2. _____ 5. _____
3. _____ 6. _____

Choose **1** name from your list of "Fairy Tale Names" and describe that character.

Name of character: _____

Descriptive Words:

1. _____ 4. _____
2. _____ 5. _____
3. _____ 6. _____

Choose **1** name from your list of "Hollywood Names" and describe that character.

Name of character: _____

Descriptive Words:

1. _____ 4. _____
2. _____ 5. _____
3. _____ 6. _____

and they lived...

Choose **2** characters from your lists. Answer these questions about them in a few sentences:

1- Where do they live? Do they live together?

2- How did they meet? How long have they known each other?

3- What makes them the same? What about them is different? Be sure you are considering their descriptions.

4- What adventures have they had together?

13

Synonym for "Said"...

Below is a list of synonyms for the word "said." How many more can you add?

1. spoke
2. uttered
3. recited
4. gabbed
5. stated
6. declared
7. told
8. mentioned
9. muttered
10. discussed

11. _____
12. _____
13. _____
14. _____
15. _____
16. _____
17. _____
18. _____
19. _____
20. _____
21. _____
22. _____
23. _____
24. _____
25. _____
26. _____
27. _____
28. _____
29. _____
30. _____
31. _____
32. _____
33. _____
34. _____
35. _____
36. _____

wonderful words...

What is a wonderful word?

A- A word that is different (you don't hear it all the time).

B- A word that sounds nice to listen to.

C- A word that "draws a picture" in your mind.

1. Start a "wonderful word" list. When you read or you hear someone use a "wonderful word," write it on your list. (Write the meaning of the word if you don't know what it means.)

2. Pick a word that you like. Write it down and list as many words as you can think of that mean the same thing. Example: BIG : large/giant/huge...

3. Write a poem using words from your "wonderful word list" only. Don't worry if what you write doesn't make sense--instead, put words together by how they sound.

Super Sentences...

Sentences are like blocks, you need them to "build" a story--or anything you want to write.

How to write super sentences:

A- Use describing words. Instead of: She had chocolate cake and a glass of milk, how about: She had a gooey hunk of chocolate cake and an ice cold glass of milk.

B- Use interesting action words. Instead of: The boy ran, how about: The boy galloped.

C- Ask yourself: Is this the best way I can say what I mean?

Look through some books in your classroom or school library. Find 5 sentences that you think are super. Copy them. Tell someone what you think is super about each one.

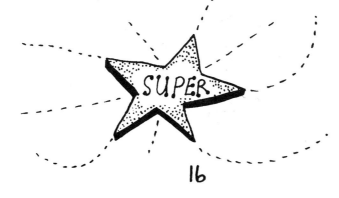

16

1st Things 1st ooo

THE MORE YOU KNOW ABOUT A THING THE EASIER IT WILL BE TO WRITE ABOUT.

To describe something you need to look at it <u>very</u> <u>carefully</u> and write down what you see. The more things you "tell," the easier it is for people to **see** what you are writing about. <u>Example</u>: A ball is on the table ➡ A large blue rubber ball with silver stars is on the kitchen table.

It take <u>time</u> to see things. When you look at something, let your eyes move S-L-O-W-L-Y around the thing — up⬆, down⬇, from side to side. ↩

🔲 Pick a small object in your classroom. Put it in front of you. Look at it and answer each question.

• What color (or colors) is it?

• What shape is it?

• What is its size and weight?

• What is it made of?

• How many parts does it have?

• What sounds can it make?

• What does it do?

• Can it be taken apart?

• What does it look like on the inside?

• Does it have anything that makes it different from all other ones like it? (Like a scratch or dent)

↓ MYSTERY OBJECT

17

description checklist ✔

Check out these things when you want to write a description.

people.
height
weight
hair color
hair style
eye color
shape of nose
shape of mouth
teeth (braces, missing...)
complexion
birthmarks, freckles
fingernails
jewelry worn
clothing (style, color)
type of walk
voice (loud, accent)
age
personality (shy, friendly)

places
sounds in the place
smells
things
climate/temperature
colors
shape
height
width
the way the outside looks
the way the inside looks
where the place is
what is it near
what is it next to
mood
people in the place (who)
number of people
building materials (brick, etc.)

objects
color
shape
size
weight
texture
what it does
temperature of object

smell
taste
sound it makes
how many parts it has
how it works
what it's made out of
can it be taken apart
what the inside looks like.

18

keep on looking...

1 Look around your classroom and make a list of all the __blue__ things you see. When you finish, compare your list with someone else.

2 Hold your hands in front of you. Make a list of the differences between your right hand and your left hand.

3 __Without__ looking, write the answers to these questions:

- What color are your teachers' eyes?
- Does your school's front door swing in or out?
- How many bulletin boards are in your classroom?
- Where is the nearest fire extinguisher?
- What color are the walls in your cafeteria?

When you finish, check your answers.

19

Early Childhood...

Most people have heard:

"STICKS AND STONES CAN BREAK MY BONES BUT NAMES CAN NEVER HURT ME."

and

"IF YOU CAN'T SAY SOMETHING NICE ABOUT SOMEONE, DON'T SAY ANYTHING AT ALL."

Based on <u>your</u> experience, write about whether or not these are true.

noticing things...

Sometimes, you can "see" <u>without</u> looking.

1- Close your eyes and listen to the sounds in your classroom. List as many as you can.

2- Drink some water. In a few sentences, describe what it tastes like.

3- With your teacher's permission, go to the school cafeteria at lunchtime and make a list of all the different smells you smell.

4- Besides your eyes, what can you "see" with? Make a list.

Falling leaves are like silver dollars...

One way to write a description is to <u>compare</u> one thing to another thing: snow <u>is like</u> vanilla ice cream, television <u>is like</u> a window.

1- Finish these descriptions:

Rubber bands are like...   A spoon is like...

Chocolate is like...   A balloon is like...

Sneakers are like...   A sneeze is like...

A clock is like...   Paint is like...

A diamond is like...   Being scared is like...

2- Pick an object in your classroom. Put it in front of you. Make a list of all of its parts. (Example: book → pages, cover, words, ink, pictures...) Use this list to write a poem about your object.

:POEM:
Pages are like...
A cover is like...
Words are like...
Ink is like...
Pictures are like...
<u>A book</u> is like...

II. getting to know me

What I Think...

inside-out...

1- Write a few sentences about yourself but don't talk about what you look like on the outside. Instead, write about what you are like on the inside - your feelings, your likes and dislikes, and what you know.

2- Turn something inside-out. (Suggestions: an article of clothing, a paper bag, a pencil case). When you turn something inside-out, what can you learn? Write your answer in one or two sentences.

3- Make a list of words that describe the "inside" you. Make another list of words that describe the "outside" you.

What is a smile? List some things that make you smile. When is it hard for you to smile?

How can you make someone else smile? Where do you feel your smile? Answer these questions in a few sentences.

the name game ooo

1- Pick a <u>new</u> first name for yourself. Write a note to someone and tell him what you like about your "new" name.

2- Practice writing your new name in a lot of different ways:

large · cursive · slowly · with chalk · sloppy · in pencil · in ink · with crayons · fancy · printing · fast · tiny · with paint · with felt tip markers · on the blackboard · plain · backwards

3- I wish my real first name could mean

_____ because _____ .

27

angry...

1- Make a list of things that make you angry.

2- What does anger feel like? Write your answer in one or two sentences.

3- When I get angry, I _____.

4- How can you stop a fight from beginning? Make a poster with your suggestions.

5- The best thing to do after a fight is.....

6- Write one sentence that "**S-H-O-U-T-S!**"

7- When someone shouts at me, I feel...

another way...

Another way to "describe" is to tell what things <u>feel</u> like.

1. Touch your hair. Write a sentence that tells how your hair feels.

2. Put your hand over your heart. What do you feel? Write one sentence about it.

3. Walk barefoot on the floor of your classroom. What do your feet feel when they touch the floor?

4. Touch the clothes you are wearing. Describe the way your clothes feel.

5. Write a poem about things you <u>can't</u> touch. Start each line with: I can't touch...

the magical mystery cure...

Pretend that you are the famous Dr. Fixit and you have the power to cure everything. Write some prescriptions for:

- loneliness
- sadness
- anger
- unhappiness
- crying
- a broken heart

Write your prescriptions on special sheets that look like this:

> **Rx** If you _are lonely_
> then _____
> _____
>
> Dr. Fixit, M.D.

Say ahhh...

reflections of me...

1- Look at yourself in a mirror. Write a poem about what you see. Look in the mirror while you are writing.

2- How are you the <u>same</u> as everyone else? How are you <u>different</u> from everyone else? List as many things as you can think of.

3- Finish this sentence:

One thing I would like to change about myself is _____

heart to heart...

1- Think about these different kinds of hearts:

- a heart of gold
- a heartache
- a cold heart
- a broken heart
- a heartburn
- a heart in your mouth
- a big heart
- a heart of stone

Pick <u>one</u> and in a few sentences tell what you think it would feel like to have that kind of heart.

2- Sit quietly for a few minutes. Listen to what your heart is trying to tell you. Draw an outline of your heart and fill it with the words that "come from your heart.

3- Can hearts talk? Fill in the blanks:

Sometimes my head tells me to _____ but my heart says _____.

32

yes, i can...

1- What are some of the ways you take care of yourself at school? Write some sentences that start:

At school, I can _____.

2- What are some of the ways you take care of yourself at home? Write some sentences that start:

At home, I can_____.

3- List <u>four</u> things that you would like to do for yourself that you can't do now.

4- Finish these sentences:

• When I do something by myself, I...

• Most people don't think I can...

• The hardest thing I ever learned to do was...

• Sometimes, I wish I didn't know how to...

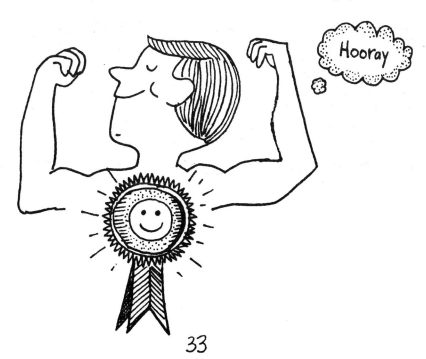

the thank you book...

Sit quietly for a few minutes and think about all the people who do nice things for you. Pick four or five people you would like to thank, name them, and in a few sentences, tell why you are thanking them. Use one sheet of paper for each person. When you finish, staple your pages into a book.

Say thank you to someone today

hooray for kids...

Answer these questions in a few sentences:

1- What's great about being a child?

2- How do you know when you're grown-up?

3- Besides age, what are the differences between kids and adults? Make a list.

4- What are some things you wish adults would remember about kids?

win or lose...

Answer one of these questions in a few sentences:

1- What is the best thing you've ever won?

or

What is the worst thing you've ever lost?

2- List three words that describe the way you act when you win

or

Write something you say to yourself when you lose

or

3- Ask some people (kids __and__ adults) this question: Can someone lose and still be a winner? Write a short note to yourself about what you find out.

it's cooking...

Friendship is a recipe made up of many different ingredients. Write your special recipe for friendship (like two cups of honesty, plus one tablespoon of fun...) When you finish, trade recipes with someone.

Teacher: Individual recipes can be combined into a class cookbook.

don'ts...

Often, grownups ask kids the question:

"What do you want to be when you grow up?"

Just this once, answer <u>this</u> question instead:

"What <u>don't</u> you want to be when you grow up?"

Answer this question in a few sentences. Tell what you <u>don't</u> want to be and then explain why.

Hmm...

<u>Teacher:</u> This activity can be expanded to include "What <u>didn't</u> you do on your summer vacation," "How <u>don't</u> you feel today?" etc.

the living room...

1. Pick <u>three</u> things in your room that could tell someone who you are. Name each thing and tell why you chose it.

2. If your room could talk, what would it say? Write a conversation that might take place between your room and you. Start like this:

    My room said, "_____".
    Then I said, "_____".

favorite things...

1. Write <u>one</u> sentence that tells your favorite:
   - breakfast food
   - game
   - place
   - month
   - time of day
   - name

2. Ask four people to name their favorite things. (Use the list in question #1). Write down what they tell you.

3. Write a two sentence note to yourself about why people have <u>different</u> favorite things.

think about it...

1- Make a list of ⑤ things you think about often.

2- When do you do your best thinking? Where do you do your best thinking? Answer these questions in a few sentences.

3- Write a letter to someone telling them about the most <u>unusual</u> thought you've ever had.

it's a date...

Pick one famous person whom you would like to invite to lunch.

1- Write a few sentences that tell whom you would pick and why you would like to have lunch with that person.

2- Write two questions that you would like to ask your guest.

3- List two things that you would tell your guest about yourself.

4- Write a menu for your luncheon. Write it on a sheet of paper that looks like this:

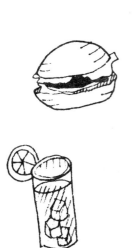

~MENU~

PREPARED BY ____(your name)____

FOR ___(your guest's name)___

?

hooray for me...

1- Spend some time looking at ads in magazines or newspapers. Pay attention to how they are written and what they say.

2- On an index card, write an ad for yourself, describing something you do very well. It can be **ANYTHING** from baking terrific peanut butter cookies, to having beautiful handwriting, to being the fastest runner in your class!

3- Take part in an "I'm-Great-At-That" Trade-off. Put your card in a special place (check with your teacher). Answer at least <u>one</u> ad for something you'd like to know how to do. Be prepared to teach what you do well in case somebody answers your ad !!!

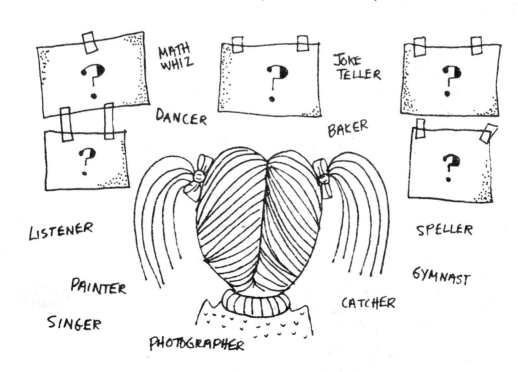

MATH WHIZ

JOKE TELLER

DANCER

BAKER

LISTENER

SPELLER

PAINTER

GYMNAST

SINGER

CATCHER

PHOTOGRAPHER

hall of fame...

Who would you put in your <u>own</u> Hall of Fame?

Pick three people (famous <u>or</u> not famous) to induct into your Hall of Fame.

Name the people you would pick and tell what they have done to deserve this honor.

two feet...

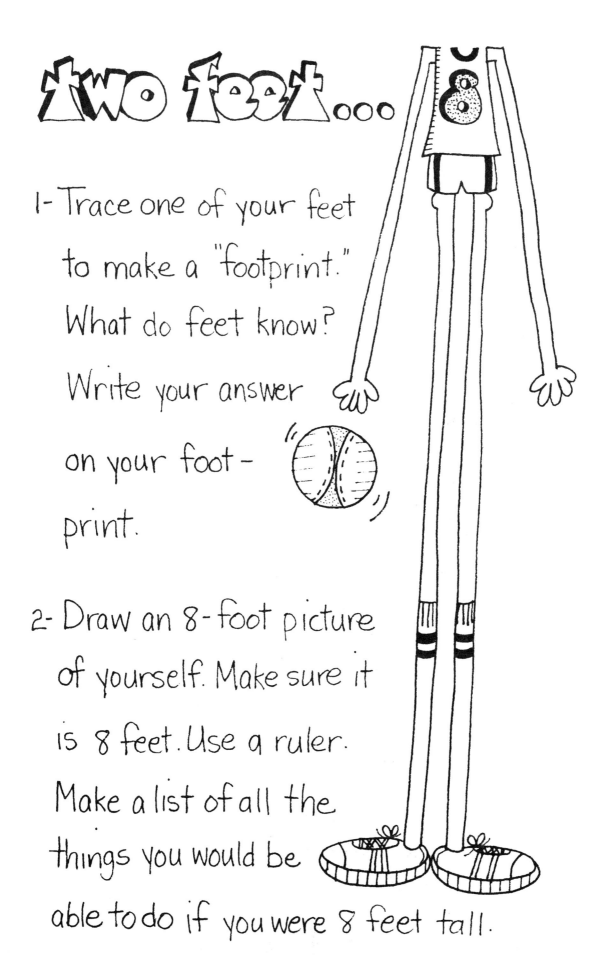

1- Trace one of your feet to make a "footprint." What do feet know? Write your answer on your foot-print.

2- Draw an 8-foot picture of yourself. Make sure it is 8 feet. Use a ruler. Make a list of all the things you would be able to do if you were 8 feet tall.

III. explorations

Discovering Others and the World...

on top of spaghetti

1- Look up "spaghetti" in the encyclopedia. Write a short report that answers these questions:

- Where does spaghetti come from?
- How is spaghetti made?

2- Finish these sentences:

Spaghetti looks like...   Spaghetti tastes like...

Spaghetti feels like...   Spaghetti smells like...

3- Do you know a really good way to eat spaghetti? (So it ends up in your mouth and _not_ on the floor!) First, write your idea in a few sentences. Then, interview 2 or 3 people and write down what they tell you.

4- Write your favorite Spaghetti and ____?____ recipe.

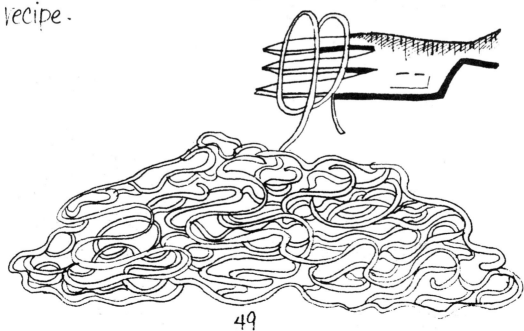

hats off to you...

1- Get some magazines and cut out a lot of different hats. Paste them on a piece of paper. Look at your "hat collage" and make a list of all the things a hat can tell you.

2- Trace the cartoon below. What do you think the hats are saying to each other? Fill in the dialogue balloons.

Bye Bye...

1- If you could go anywhere in the world, what places would you go to? Make a list.

2- You will need a <u>passport</u> for your trip. To make your passport, take 5 medium-size pieces of paper and fold them in half. Staple the pages together ••↑  List important facts about yourself on the first page, like: your birthdate, height, weight, address. On the same page, draw a picture of yourself. Leave the rest of the pages blank. The blank pages are for stamps or symbols of the places you want to visit. Look in the encyclopedia or an atlas to find out about the places on your list. Pick out something important about each place and draw your symbol.

3- What did you miss while you were away? Answer this question in a few sentences.

who's who ...

Who is: Cleopatra?

Clark Gable?

Mata Hari?

Napoleon?

Millard Fillmore?

Have you heard of these people? If you have, write down what you know. If you haven't heard of them, choose **two** of the names and make up things about them. Answer these questions in a few sentences:

- What does this person look like? (Draw a picture too.)

- Where does this person live?

- What is this person's job?

When you finish writing, look up the people you chose in an encyclopedia and find out who they are.

52

shoes to boot...

1- Make a list of all the different kinds of shoes you have seen. Trade lists with someone. Read their list.

2- Describe a pair of shoes that are in your classroom now. Use your description checklist.

3- What are your favorite shoes? (Shoes you own now, shoes you used to own, or shoes you dream of owning.) In a few sentences, describe these shoes and tell what makes them special.

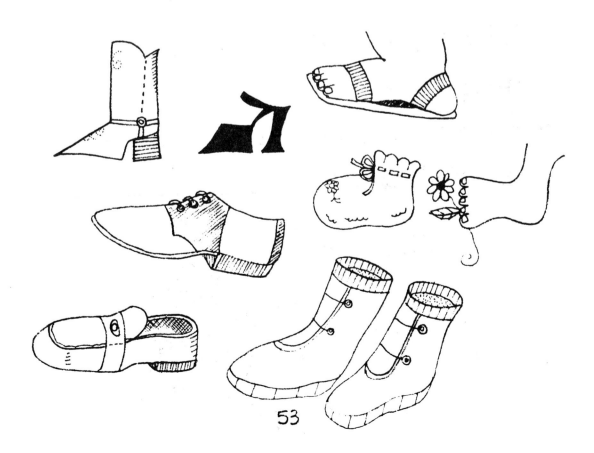

teach me...

Answer these questions in a few sentences:

1-What is a teacher?

2-How is a teacher like/different from a parent?

3-How does someone get to be a teacher? (Ask 2 or 3 teachers in your school. Write down what you find out.)

4-What are some of the things a teacher does? Make a list. When you finish your list, ask your teacher to tell you the things s/he does.

5- Finish this sentence: I was surprised to learn that teachers _____.

hiccups...

In a few sentences, describe what a hiccup feels like.

Make a poster that lists some ways to make hiccups go away. (Things that you have tried or that you have heard about.)

hiccup!

dog days...

1. What are the differences between a <u>toy</u> dog and a <u>live</u> dog? Make a list.

Toy Dog	Live Dog
1.	1.
2.	2.
3.	3.

LIKE THIS

2. Are both the toy dog and the live dog REAL or, is only <u>one</u> of them real? Write 2-3 sentences about this.

3. Which would you rather have — a toy dog or a live dog? Why? Answer this question in a few sentences.

Woof

DOG

the big cheese...

1- Look up "cheese" in an encyclopedia to find out how cheese is made. Write 3 or 4 sentences about what you find out.

2- Ask <u>ten</u> people to name their favorite cheese. Make a chart that shows the results.

3- Write a poem about <u>four</u> or more of these cheeses:

- Gouda
- Swiss
- Cheddar
- Brie
- Cream Cheese

- American
- Roquefort
- Meunster
- Edam
- Cottage Cheese

If you haven't eaten some of these cheeses, make up things about them for your poem.

57

the new word dictionary

Our language has many words in it but sometimes new words need to be made up to name new inventions or new things. Pretend that you are writing a dictionary and you need to make up names for each of the imaginary things listed below:

1- Shoes that help people walk on water.

2- A breakfast cereal made from flowers.

3- A book that you can eat when you are done reading it.

4- Shoelaces that tie by themselves.

5- A candy bar that gets rid of the hiccups.

6- A mirror that can be fixed to make a person look ten pounds heavier or ten pounds lighter.

7- A person whose job it is to collect and study rainbows.

Make some dictionary pages - write the names you make up and copy the definitions.

58

law and order...

1- Write one sentence that tells what a law is.

2- Finish this sentence: A law is like a promise because _____.

3- Write a law that you think would help children.

4- Why do people need laws? Talk this over with some of your classmates. Then, write one or two sentences that tell why you think people need laws.

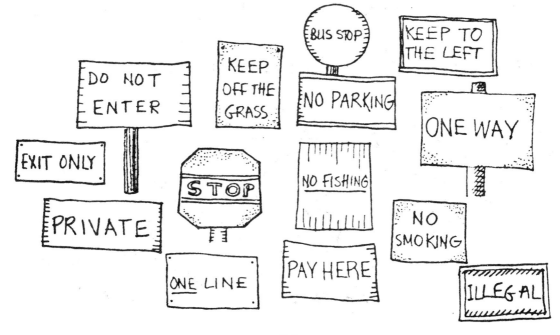

the word game...

1- Without looking in the dictionary, write what you think these words mean:

- sygzy
- noxious
- zephr

When you are done, look them up and find out if you were right.

2- Make up a word. Spell it and give it a meaning. Trade words with someone and use your partner's word in a sentence.

60

IV. imagination

Tradition With A Twist...

help, i'm trapped in a baby food jar!

Close your eyes and pretend that you are trapped inside a baby food jar. Answer these questions in a few sentences:

1- What is it like in there?

2- Where is the jar?

3- How did you get in the jar?

4- What are you doing to keep busy while you are inside?

5- How do you plan to get out?

HOORAY!

63

surprise₀₀₀

Write a short letter to a friend about the time...

- Big Bird was your Substitute Teacher

or

- Spiderman was your Substitute Teacher

or

- Snoopy was your Substitute Teacher

Choose <u>one</u>. In your letter, tell:

How you felt when you found out...

What happened during class...

One special thing you will always remember...

Some things you said...

The first person you told after school...

Start your letter this way ➡

DEAR (your friends' name)

GUESS WHAT!

64

HOW DO YOU SAY HELLO TO A GHOST?

Pretend you are Professor I.M. Spooky from Trannsylvania College. You have studied ghosts for many years and now you have been asked to talk about "How You Say Hello To A Ghost." You have been studying this for a long time, so you know at least three or four ways. Start your speech like this: "Ladies and Gentlemen, when you want to say hello to a ghost, you must..."

my pet monster...

1- Draw a picture of your pet monster.

2- What foods does a pet monster eat ? Make a grocery list.

3- Make a Pet Monster Manual. Use the picture you made for the front cover. Staple five sheets of paper to the picture to make a book. On each sheet write special hints for the care and feeding of a pet monster, like:
- tricks you can teach a pet monster.
- the kind of exercise a pet monster needs.
- what to do if a pet monster gets sick.
- how often a pet monster needs to be fed and walked.

4- Write a poem about what it would be like to have a pet monster.

66

conversations with a gorilla...

One day I was walking down the street and this big, hairy gorilla came up to me and tapped me on the shoulder.

He said, "_____."

Then I said, "_____"

Fill in the blanks and add as many blanks as you need to finish your story.

howdy!

a handy story...

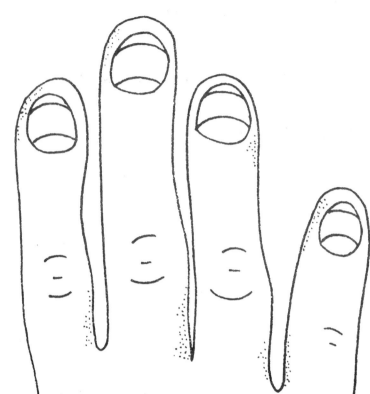

Pretend that your hands can talk. Trace your hands on a piece of paper and then write a conversation between your left hand and your right hand. Write the things your left hand says on the drawing of your left hand. Write the things your right hand says on the drawing of your right hand.

the galloping gourmet

Pretend you are a famous chef. You are preparing Mystery Stew. Trace this recipe card and make a list of ingredients for your stew. Pairs of ingredients <u>must</u> <u>rhyme</u>.

MYSTERY STEW

1. HAM AND JAM

2. GOATS AND COATS

3.

4.

5.

6.

7.

8.

9.

10.

11.

12.

When you finish, turn your card over and write a recipe for Mystery Stew using your list of ingredients.

who knows?

Ask three people <u>one</u> of these questions:
- How did the stars get into the sky?
- Why do people stop growing?

Write down what they tell you. Add your <u>own</u> answer and make them into a book called, "Who Knows?" Use one page for each answer.

Forgotten Things

Remember some of the poems you have heard or read... what were they about? Make a list in your mind.

Write a poem about something that people <u>don't</u> usually write poems about.

Start your poem this way:

- Nobody writes poems about ___(you fill in)___.

Hmm...

?

Aaron Zwieback's amazing box of cookies

Aaron Zwieback shares the secret of his
amazing box of cookies with you:

 If you eat the chocolate chip cookie,
you glow in the dark.

 If you eat the peanut butter cookie,
you become invisible.

 If you eat the oatmeal cookie,
you grow to be 8 feet tall.

 If you eat the fig newton, you
become the smartest person on
earth for one hour.

Write a short story about a time you ate
one of Aaron Zwieback's cookies. Tell which
cookie you ate, and then tell all the things that
happened to you.

mystery foot...

Imagine that you found this footprint in your room ➡

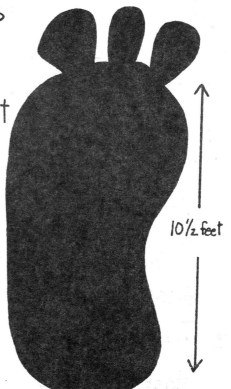

10½ feet

Write a news bulletin about this footprint. Answer these questions in your bulletin:

1- Whose footprint is it ?

2- How did it get in your room ?

3- What are you going to do about it ?

4- Where is the footprint-maker now ?

Start your news bulletin this way:

"We interrupt the following program to bring you this special message! A footprint measuring 10½ feet long has just been spotted in ___(your name)___ 's bedroom!"

When you finish writing, tape record your news bulletin.

the Undersea Creep

Down below in the ocean deep, lives a wonderful creature called the Undersea Creep!

1. Describe the Undersea Creep.

2. Write _two_ questions about the Undersea Creep that you would like to know the answers to.

3. Trade questions with someone in your class. In a few sentences, answer your classmate's questions about the Undersea Creep.

Teacher: Combine the answers into a class story called "The Legend of the Undersea Creep". Duplicate for home reading.

V. mystery chapter

One-of-a-kind Assignments...

then what?

1- What would happen if there were <u>no telephones</u>? List as many things as you can think of that would happen if this was true.

2- What would happen if it <u>NEVER rained</u>? List as many things as you can think of that would happen if this was true.

3- What would happen if there was <u>no paper</u>? List as many things as you can think of that would happen if this was true.

No telephones? then People who print telephone books would be out of business...

the incredibly delicious and long sandwich list...

Make a list of <u>ten</u> incredibly yummy sandwich combinations to put between two slices of bread, like:

• tuna and raisins and walnuts and celery

• peanut butter and banana slices and maple syrup and chocolate chips

• cream cheese and apple slices and cinammon

<u>Teacher</u>: Compile the lists and post where everyone can see it. Have fun reading it and suggest that students copy several combinations (to take home) that they'd like to try.

sunny days...

Have you ever tried to get to Sesame Street? Where do you think it is and how would you get there?

Write directions that tell how to get to Sesame Street.

When you finish writing, make a map to go with your directions.

SESAME STREET

the book of lists ...
✳ CLASS ACTIVITY

Ask each student to make a list of the five:

- best flavors of ice cream ...
- most beautiful things in the world ...
- best T.V. shows ...
- best ages to be ...
- nicest first names ...
- most beautiful colors ...
- things most people own ...
- best foods ...
- hardest things to do ...
- most famous people ...

- nicest places ...
- best fruits ...
- best months ...
- best pets ...
- most awful foods ...
- best stories ...
- greatest people ...
- things everyone needs ...
- best cartoons ...
- ? ? ? (make up one!)

Choose the number of categories depending on time and class ability.

Collect the lists and duplicate.

Provide time for students to read and compare.

Process this activity by leading a discussion on differences/similarities in the way people "see" things. Ask students to complete these sentence stems: I learned... I wonder about... I was surprised...

mini-books ooo

A mini-book is a <u>very</u> small book.

How to make a mini-book:

1- Cut out ten pieces of plain paper. Make the paper two inches tall and three inches wide. Use a ruler!

2- One piece of paper will be the cover. Put the title of the story on the cover.

3- The rest of the paper will be the pages in the book. In a mini-book, write <u>one</u> sentence at the bottom of each page. The rest of the space is for a picture.

4- Use as many pieces of paper as you need to write your story. When you finish, staple your book together.

5- Use <u>one</u> of these titles for your mini-book:
- Pow!
- Abracadabra!
- Shazam!
- Wow!
- Oops!

the child's book of MONSTERS

You will need one sheet of paper for each letter of the alphabet. Starting with "A", make up the name of a monster (example: The Amazing Atomic Monster). Write the monster's name at the top of the page. Next, write a few sentences about the monster. Tell what the monster looks like, where the monster lives, what foods the monster eats, and any special powers the monster has. When you finish writing about the monster, draw a picture of the monster. Then, work on the next page and the next letter. When you finish the whole alphabet, staple your pages into a book.

the crazy book...

Think about something absolutely CRAZY?

Like... a pink and orange striped elephant
        eating a chocolate ice cream cone!

Think of some more crazy things. Make a book
like this:

staple →

HA

HA

HA

Did you ever see a pink and orange striped
elephant eating a chocolate ice cream cone?

staple →

Write one crazy thing per page.

When you finish your book, share it
with someone.

ice cream... ⌒⌒

BASKET ROBINS (31) FLAVOR LIST

1. Ambrosia
2. Cookie Crunch
3. Jamoca
4. Rocky Road
5. Cola Nut
6. Butter Pecan
7. French Vanilla
8. English Toffee
9. Banana Cake
10. Lemon Chiffon
11. Fudge Brownie
12. Date Krunch
13. Cherry Vanilla
14. Orange
15. Lemon Swirl
16. Grape Fiz
17. Strawberry Ice
18. Cherry Pie
19. Gingerbread
20. Fudge Ripple
21. Marshmallow
22. Nutcracker Sweet
23. Bosten Cream Pie
24. Peanut Butter
25. Chocolate Ribbon
26. Maple Nut
27. Chocolate Cheesecake
28. Pistachio Almond
29. Peppermint
30. Fruit Tree
31. M&M Vanilla
?

1 Make up <u>five</u> flavors to add to the flavor list.

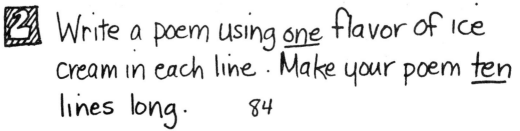
2 Write a poem using <u>one</u> flavor of ice cream in each line. Make your poem <u>ten</u> lines long.

84

Magic Writing...

Magic Writing is done with pictures. You make a picture that starts with the same letter as each of the letters in the word you want to write. Like:

carrot

apple

television

C   **A**   **T**

1- Write your name in Magic Writing.

2- Write a <u>short</u> message to someone using Magic Writing.

3- Is Magic Writing a good way to write? Why or why not? Answer this question in a few sentences.

4- Make up your own writing system. Make a list of the things you need to know <u>before</u> you begin.

5- Just for fun, write:

SUPERCALIFRAGILISTICEXPIALADOCIOUS in Magic Writing!

the dream...

✳ CLASS ACTIVITY

Teacher: Ask each student to complete <u>one</u>

GREAT sentence starting with the words:

AND THEN I...

Make sure that no one knows what anyone else is writing. When everyone is finished, collect the sentences.

Teacher begins the dream:

"I was in my flying washing machine when I saw a purple cow water skiing in the atlantic Ocean..."

Read all the student's sentences aloud.

mystery metal writing...

ALUMINUM FOIL ↓

Meet me at midnight

*hold this message up to a mirror!

1- Get a piece of aluminum foil and place it shiny side up.

2- Use a __dull__ pencil to write a one-sentence secret message.

3- Turn your message over (so the dull side is up) and tape it to a piece of paper.

4- Pass it to a friend (your friend needs to hold your message in front of a mirror).

5- Okay friend, you write a message back!

that's a scream!

Make a book called:

ha ha ha

Write down some of your favorite jokes and stories. Use one page for each joke.

Draw a picture to go along with what you write.

When you finish, share your book with someone you'd like to see smile.

giggle

What did one banana say to the other banana?

'tis the season...

Teacher: Divide your class the following way: all children with birthdays in September, October, November → Fall Group; December, January, February → Winter Group; March, April, May → Spring Group; June, July, August → Summer Group.

1. Make a list of all the things you know about that happen in your birthday's season. Suggestions: holidays (use an almanac or calender); events (school starts, daylight savings time begins, trees begin to bud...); average temperature; recreational activities for the season.

2. What do you like most about your season? Why? What do you like least about your season? Why? Answer BOTH these questions in a few sentences.

3. Cut out a very large circle from light-colored construction paper. This will be the top of your birthday cake for your season. Decorate (paint, markers, crayons, glitter...) your birthday cake so that it tells something about your season.

4. Share your findings and "cake" with your class.

89

giant postcard from OUTER SPACE

Teacher: Make a dittomaster that looks like this ↓

⚹ DRAW SO POSTCARD MEASURES 8½ X 11. GIANT POSTCARDS ARE ALSO GREAT FOR SOCIAL STUDIES UNITS.

Dear _____,

Hi, I'm on _____.

I saw _____

_____

_____

                from,

_____

OUTER SPACE
AM
FILL IN THE DATE

25¢

·GIANT POSTCARD·

TO:

_____

_____

_____

Air MAIL

✂ CLIP AND SAVE ↗

- -

From this list of planets, pick <u>one</u> that you would like to visit: Venus   Mars   Jupiter

Mercury   Pluto   Neptune

Saturn   Uranus

Look in the encyclopedia to find out some things about the planet you picked. Then, write a GIANT POSTCARD to someone about the planet you are "Visiting." Turn the postcard over and draw a picture of one of the sights to see.

90

the fortune cookie factory

COPY THIS SECRET RECIPE TO TRY AT HOME!

fortune cookies

ingredients:

4 Tablespoons flour
2 Tablespoons brown sugar
1 Tablespoon cornstarch
dash of salt

2 tablespoons vegetable oil
1 egg white
3 tablespoons water
½ teaspoon grated orange or lemon peel

1: In mixing bowl, stir together flour, sugar, cornstarch and salt.

2: Add oil and egg white. Stir until smooth.

3: Add water and grated peel. Stir again.

4: Grease fry pan and place over medium heat.

5: When pan is hot, drop a tablespoon of batter in it and rotate pan so batter spreads into a thin 3½ inch circle. Cook for 4 minutes, turn over, cook 2 minutes more.

6: Working quickly, remove batter with spatula, place fortune across center, fold in half, then bend the cookie slightly over the edge of a bowl. Set cookies on cookie sheet to cool.

Fortune cookies are a lot of fun. Did you ever wonder who writes the fortunes that you find inside? Today you will write fortunes for the Do-It-Yourself-Fortune-CookieFactory. A fortune tells about something that might happen in the future. Make your fortunes <u>one</u> sentence long.

First, cut some paper about this size

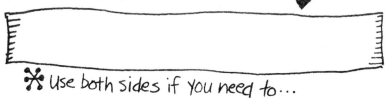

✳ Use both sides if you need to...

Next, write <u>one</u> fortune on each piece of paper. <u>Suggestions</u>: Your face will be seen on tv <u>or</u> you will find $100 by the time you are 16... When you finish, share your fortunes with your class.

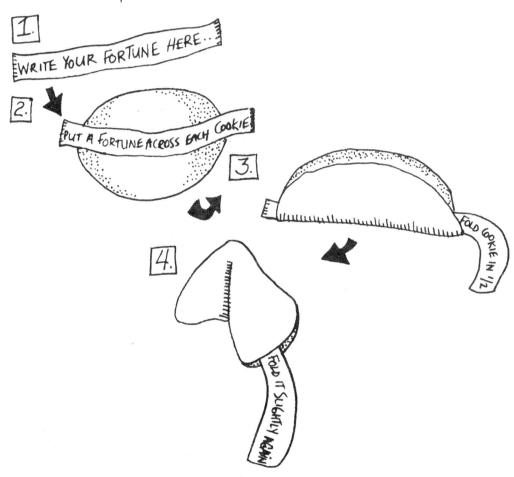

1. WRITE YOUR FORTUNE HERE...

2. PUT A FORTUNE ACROSS EACH COOKIE

3. FOLD COOKIE IN 1/2

4. FOLD IT SLIGHTLY AGAIN

<u>Teacher</u>: If time permits, make fortune cookies in class and use your students' fortunes.

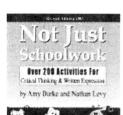

Dynamic Speakers
Creative Workshops
Relevant Topics

Nathan Levy, author of the <u>Stories with Holes</u> series and <u>There Are Those</u>, and other nationally known authors and speakers, can help your school or organization achieve positive results with children. We can work with you to provide a complete in-service package or have one of our presenters lead one of several informative and entertaining workshops.

Workshop Topics Include:

- Practical Activities for Teaching Gifted Children
Critical Thinking Skills

- Differentiating in the Regular Classroom

- How to Read, Write and Think Better

- Using <u>Stories with Holes</u> and Other Thinking Activities

- Powerful Strategies to Enhance the Learning of Your Gifted and Highly Capable Students

- Powerful Strategies to Help Your Students With Special Needs be More Successful Learners

- The Principal as an Educational Leader

and many more…

Nathan Levy, author and consultant

Nathan Levy is the author of more than 40 books which have sold almost 250,000 copies to teachers and parents in the US, Europe, Asia, South America, Australia and Africa. His unique <u>Stories with Holes</u> series continues to be proclaimed the most popular activity used in gifted, special education and regular classrooms by hundreds of educators. An extremely popular, dynamic speaker on thinking, writing and differentiation, Nathan is in high demand as a workshop leader in school and business settings. As a former school principal, company president, parent of four daughters and management trainer, Nathan's ability to transfer knowledge and strategies to audiences through humorous, thought provoking stories assures that participants leave with a plethora of new ways to approach their future endeavors.

Please write or call to receive workshop information.

NL Associates, Inc., P.O. Box 1199, Hightstown, NJ 08520-0399
(732) 656 - 7822
www.storieswithholes.com